Reading with Phonics

Reading

with Phonics

Julie Hay

Charles E. Wingo

REVISED

J. B. Lippincott Company

CHICAGO   PHILADELPHIA   NEW YORK

ABOUT THE AUTHORS

JULIE HAY: For many years Director of Primary Reading in the elementary schools—Argo, Summit, and Bedford Park, Illinois.

CHARLES E. WINGO: Professor of Education, Monmouth College, Monmouth, Illinois.

CONSULTANTS

MISS MARY HLETKO, primary teacher in the Walker School, Bedford Park, Illinois.

MRS. MARY SAMTER, Wisconsin State College, Stevens Point, Wisconsin.

Story on page 86 adapted from Lewis Carroll's *Alice in Wonderland*.

Library of Congress Catalog Card Number: 60-9599

Printed in the United States of America

a A

e E

i I

o O

u U

s S

m M

f F

r R

n N

g G

b B

t T

p P

d D

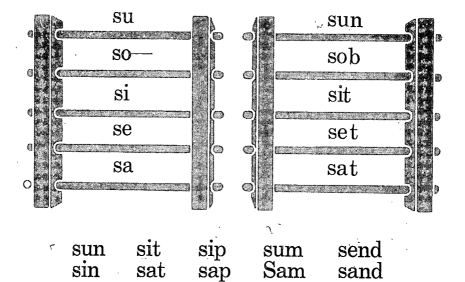

su
so—
si
se
sa

sun
sob
sit
set
sat

| sun | sit | sip | sum | send |
| sin | sat | sap | Sam | sand |

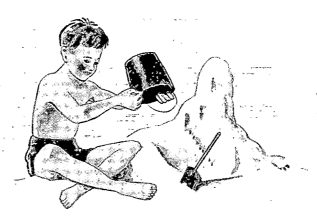

Sam sits in the sun.

He makes a sand house.

a e i o u

mu	must
mo	mop
mi	miss
me—	met
ma	man

met miss man mop mad
mat mess men map mud

Miss Muff met Miss Mop on a mat.

Miss Muff said, "Come play."

a   e   i   o   u

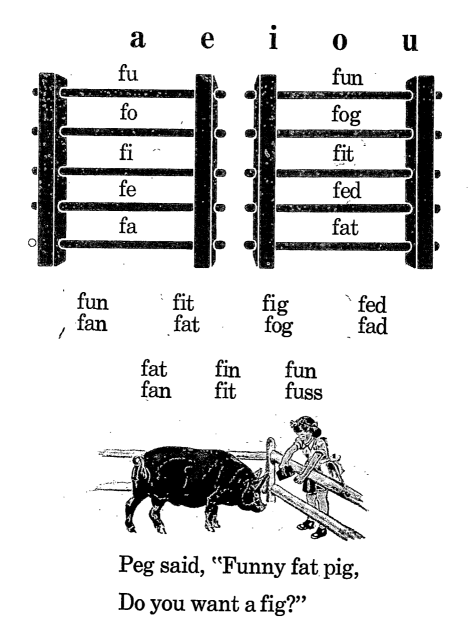

fu	fun
fo	fog
fi	fit
fe	fed
fa	fat

| fun | fit | fig | fed |
| fan | fat | fog | fad |

| fat | fin | fun |
| fan | fit | fuss |

Peg said, "Funny fat pig,

Do you want a fig?"

Peg fed four figs to the pig.

22

a　e　i　o　u

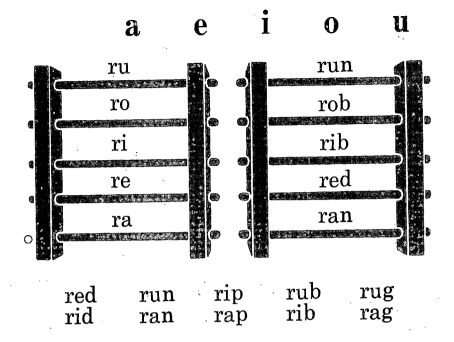

ru	run
ro	rob
ri	rib
re	red
ra	ran

| red | run | rip | rub | rug |
| rid | ran | rap | rib | rag |

Rags ran after a rat.

Rob ran after Rags.

Rob said, "Run, run, Rags!"

23

a e i o u

nu	nut
no—	not
ni	nip
ne	net
na	nap

| not | nap | nod | nut |
| net | nip | Ned | not |

Nip has Ned's cap.

He wants Ned to get up and play.

But Ned naps on and on.

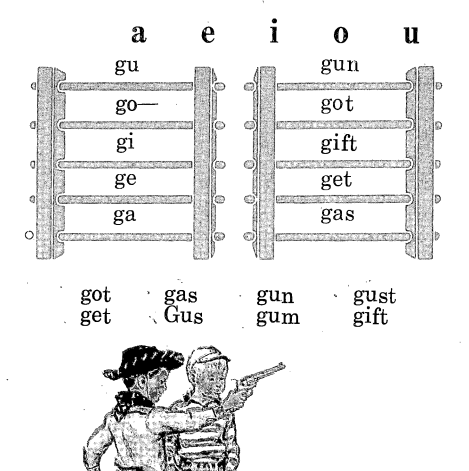

a   e   i   o   u

gu	gun
go—	got
gi	gift
ge	get
ga	gas

got	gas	gun	gust
get	Gus	gum	gift

Gus got a toy gun.

Bob said, "What a gift to get!"

Gus and Bob like toy guns.

a   e   i   o   u

bu	but
bo	Bob
bi	big
be—	bet
ba	bag

bit	bog	big	but	bed
bat	bag	beg	bet	bad

bug	bus	big
bag	but	bit

Bob said, "I like the bat and bus."

Bess said, "I like the doll bed and bib."

What gifts do you like?

a   e   i   o   u

tu	tub
to–	top
ti	tip
te	ten
ta	tap

top	ten	Tom	tan	tap
tip	tin	Tim	ten	top

Ted	tag	tot	tug	tin
ten	tap	top	tub	tip

"Put the top into my tub," said Ted.

"No," said Tom.

"I will spin my top on the tub."

27

a	e	i	o	u
sa	be	ni	bo	me
mi	ru	ma	fe	ri
ba	se	bi	ro	bu
fo	fa	si	ge	mu
na	ne	fu	to	fi
go	ga	ti	no	tu
ta	mo	re	su	so
ra	te	gu	gi	nu

set	got	gas	bit
sit	get	Gus	bet
bad	met	fun	run
bed	mat	fin	ran

Sam	must	gun	bet
sat	muss	gum	beg
fun	run	bun	tan
fuss	rug	but	tag

sat	bus	ten	tin
mat	Gus	men	fin
tag	fat	get	bed
bag	rat	net	fed

a   e   i   o   u

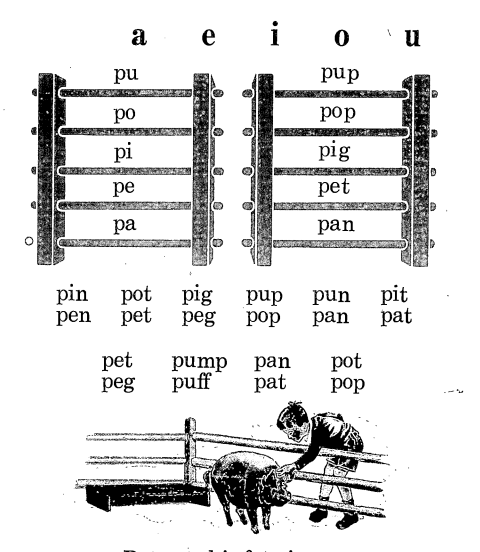

pu		pup
po		pop
pi		pig
pe		pet
pa		pan

pin	pot	pig	pup	pun	pit
pen	pet	peg	pop	pan	pat

pet	pump	pan	pot
peg	puff	pat	pop

Pat pets his fat pig.

"You are a fat pig,

But I like you," said Pat.

a   e   i   o   u

du	dug
do—	dot
di	dip
de	den
da	dad

| dug | did | Dan | Dot |
| dig | dad | den | dot |

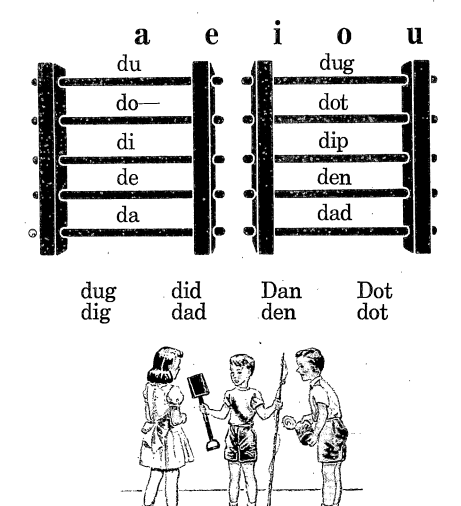

Don and Dan said,

"Come, Dot, help us dig."

"What shall we dig for?" asked Dot.

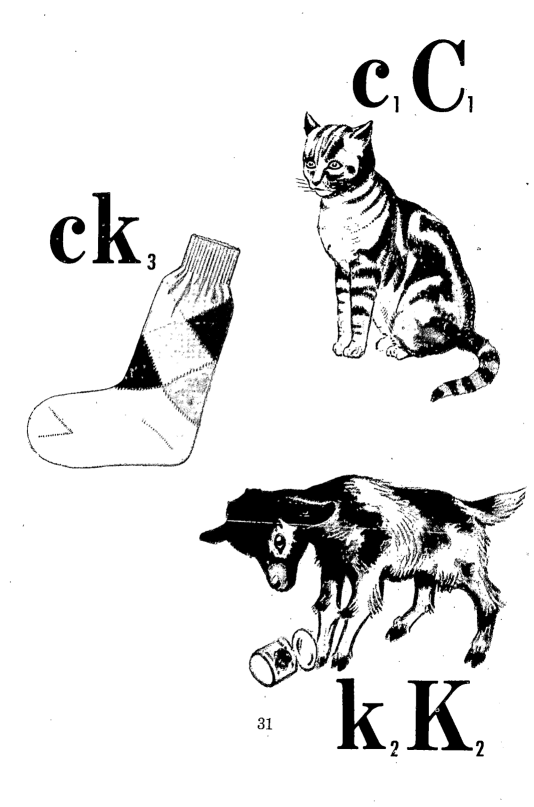

$c_1 C_1$

ck_3

$k_2 K_2$

31

a e i o u

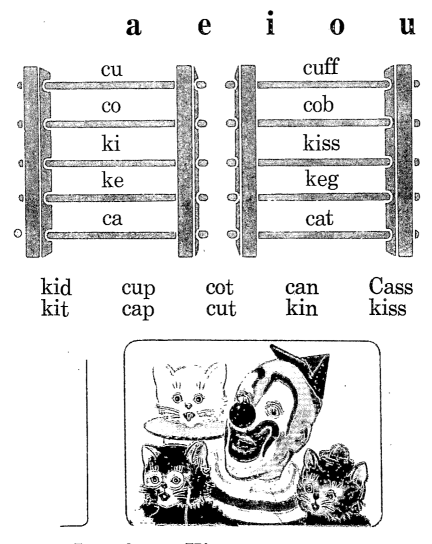

cu

cuff

co

cob

ki

kiss

ke

keg

ca

cat

| kid | cup | cot | can | Cass |
| kit | cap | cut | kin | kiss |

I am funny Kit.

I have three funny cats.

My cats and I make a funny four.

a   e   i   o   u

sick	tick	pick	rock	Dick
sack	tock	pack	rack	deck
tuck	buck	nick	suck	duck
tack	back	neck	sock	dock

pa	da	ca	po	do
de	ke	pe	du	pu
cu	pi	di	ki	co

did	pin	cat	cut
dad	pan	kit	cot
kid	cup	pot	Don
cod	cap	pat	Dan

pan	den	cot	did
pat	deck	cop	dip
pen	cat	dig	kid
pet	cap	din	kick

dad	pen	pick	dock
pad	den	Dick	rock
cat	duck	pin	did
pat	luck	kin	kid

33

l L

a   e   i   o   u

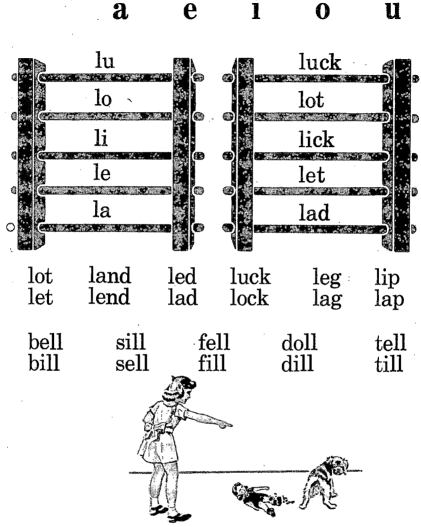

lu   luck

lo   lot

li   lick

le   let

la   lad

| lot | land | led | luck | leg | lip |
| let | lend | lad | lock | lag | lap |

| bell | sill | fell | doll | tell |
| bill | sell | fill | dill | till |

"Laddy, you are a bad pet," said Linn.

"I do not like what you did.

You bit my doll's left leg."

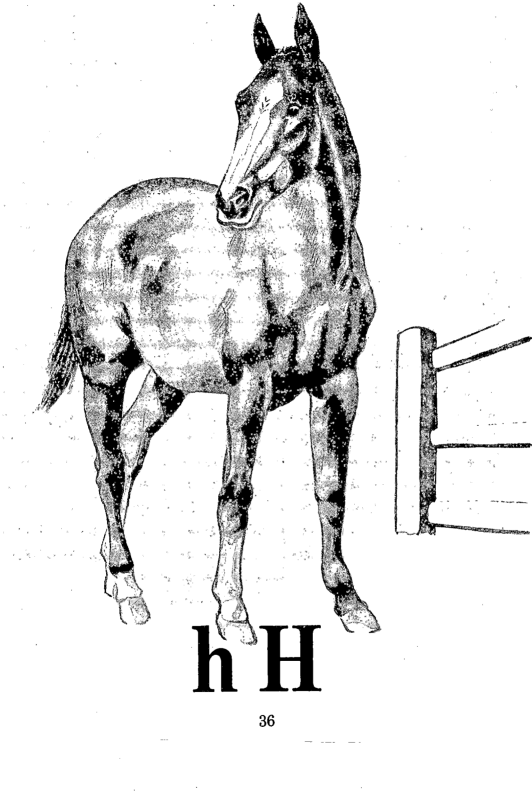

h H

a e i o u

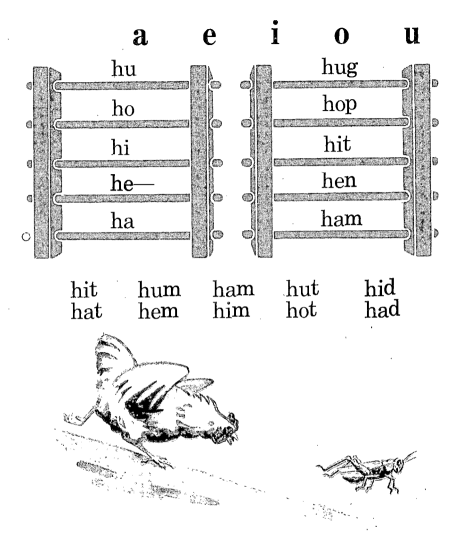

hu	hug
ho	hop
hi	hit
he—	hen
ha	ham

hit	hum	ham	hut	hid
hat	hem	him	hot	had

Hop, hop went a grasshopper down a hill.

A hungry hen ran after him.

"I will get him," said the hen.

37

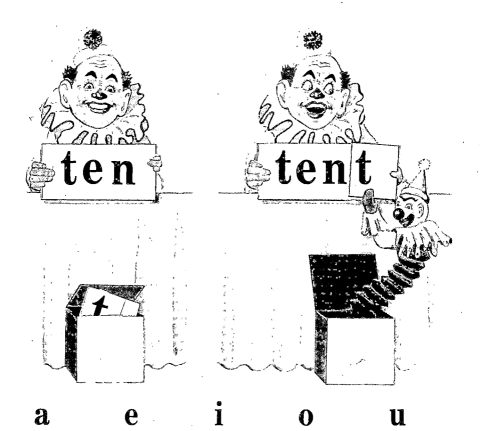

ten

tent

a	e	i	o	u
ten	mill	hum	fell	
tent	milk	hump	felt	
bum	miss	den	bell	
bump	mist	dent	belt	
sell	pan	sill	muss	
self	pant	silk	must	
Russ	men	fill	ten	
rust	mend	film	tend	

sand	lift	bend	must
send	left	band	mist
hunt	luck	land	lump
hint	lock	lend	lamp
runt	damp	pomp	fond
rent	dump	pump	fund

hand	nest	silk	lift
band	rest	milk	sift
tend	fond	sent	sack
lend	pond	bent	back
best	help	lift	rest
belt	held	list	rent

can't	dent	nest	jump
tent	camp	sift	left
duck	lump	rust	desk
bump	felt	self	kept
best	lamp	rest	luck

and	Peg	ten	fell
Nan	had	Nick	rest
self	help	Bess	lift
dad	Bob	up	dust
am	if	sell	God
Bill	in	luck	duck
Ann	must	less	rat
at	not	us	hot
best	pick	must	nest
sad	ran	back	film
can	Dan	tell	fill
man	let	hill	bus
big	red	Nan	fat
but	run	sun	rent
did	Don	sick	lock
fun	sit	kick	miss
get	tell	test	desk
got	Ted	lamp	lump

j J

a e i o u

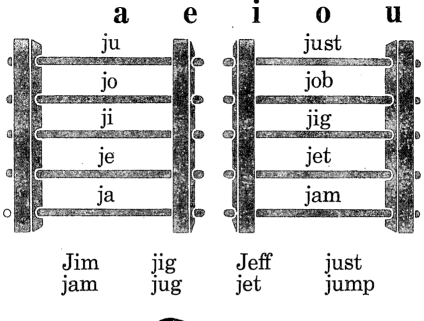

ju	just
jo	job
ji	jig
je	jet
ja	jam

Jim	jig	Jeff	just
jam	jug	jet	jump

Can you fly like a jet, jumping jack?

"No," said the jumping jack.

"I just jump up and down."

a e i o u

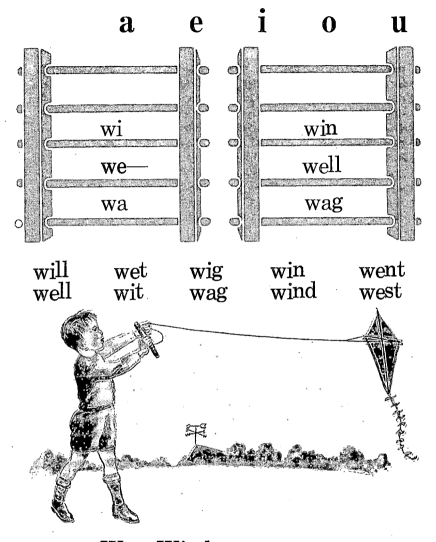

wi		win
we—		well
wa		wag

will	wet	wig	win	went
well	wit	wag	wind	west

West Wind, come.

Come and lift Will's kite.

Send it up, up into the sky.

vV

qu Qu

yY

zZ

v	qu	y	z
van	quick	yes	zip
vat	quit	yet	zest
vest	quilt	yell	buzz
vim	quack	yelp	fizz
went	quit	quill	Jess
wept	zip	jig	vest
men	just	must	wit
job	but	fizz	quilt
van	jump	fuzz	wig
yet	Jack	yelp	wag
jam	Jill	quick	west
Jim	wet	Jan	fuss
gum	well	buzz	jet
yes	wind	Jeff	web
quack	vat	jug	get
back	sick	Tess	vim
yell	sent	muss	will

sh SH

a e i o u

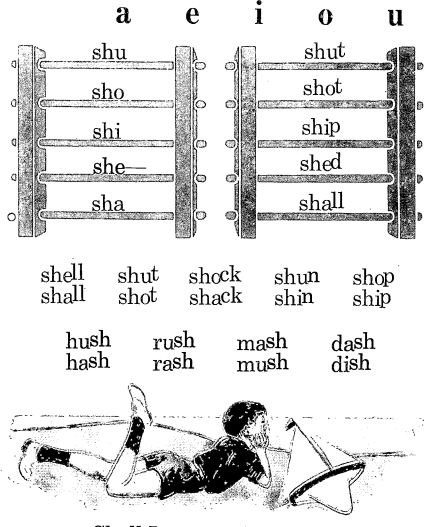

shu	shut
sho	shot
shi	ship
she—	shed
sha	shall

shell	shut	shock	shun	shop
shall	shot	shack	shin	ship

hush	rush	mash	dash
hash	rash	mush	dish

Shall I rest on the sand?

Or shall I sail my ship?

I wish I could tell what to do.

48

ch, Ch,

tch,

a e i o u

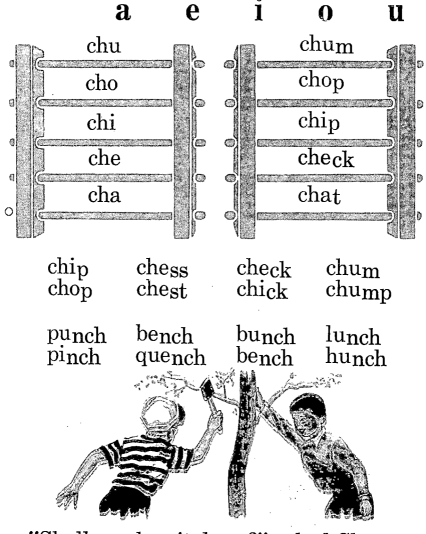

chu	chum
cho	chop
chi	chip
che	check
cha	chat

chip	chess	check	chum
chop	chest	chick	chump

punch	bench	bunch	lunch
pinch	quench	bench	hunch

"Shall we chop it down?" asked Chet.

"No, not this tree," said Chuck.

"This is a nut tree."

50

hitch	patch	Dutch	match
hatch	pitch	ditch	catch
rich	such	much	which

ng

sing	sang	ring	hang
song	sung	rang	hung
ding	wing	bang	ping
dong	king	gang	pong

nk

sink	rank	wink	tank
sank	rink	kink	bank
pink	link	chunk	bunk

th

thank	thin	thing	thud
thatch	thick	think	thump

this   thus   than   that   them   then

wh

which	when	whip	whisk

tacks	fix	ox	mix
tax	fox	ax	Max
box	six	wax	pox

at	bench	cash	dash	end
Ann	Beth	Cass	Don	Ed

fuzz	gush	hand	ink	jam
Fudd	Gus	Hank	It	Jack

king	lock	miss	nest	ox
Kit	Lad	Meg	Ned	On

path	quit	rag	six	ten
Pat	Quick	Rob	Sam	Tom

us	vest	wink	yes	zest
Up	Van	Will	Yank	Zip

top	mat	duck	path	cuff
tops	mats	ducks	paths	cuffs

Jap	Pat	Jack	Seth	Jeff
Jap's	Pat's	Jack's	Seth's	Jeff's

ship	cut	kick	song	chick
ships	cuts	kicks	songs	chicks

nest	bed	leg	king	shell
nests	beds	legs	kings	shells

Rob	Ted	Meg	Tom	Ben
Rob's	Ted's	Meg's	Tom's	Ben's

rub	nod	wag	hum	run	sing
rubs	nods	wags	hums	runs	sings

	a	**e**	**i**	**o**	**u**
1.	la	le	li	lo	lu
2.	bla	ble	bli	blo	blu
1.	la	le	li	lo	lu
2.	cla	cle	cli	clo	clu
1.	la	le	li	lo	lu
2.	fla	fle	fli	flo	flu
1.	la	le	li	lo	lu
2.	gla	gle	gli	glo	glu
1.	la	le	li	lo	lu
2.	pla	ple	pli	plo	plu
1.	la	le	li	lo	lu
2.	sla	sle	sli	slo	slu

a   e   i   o   u

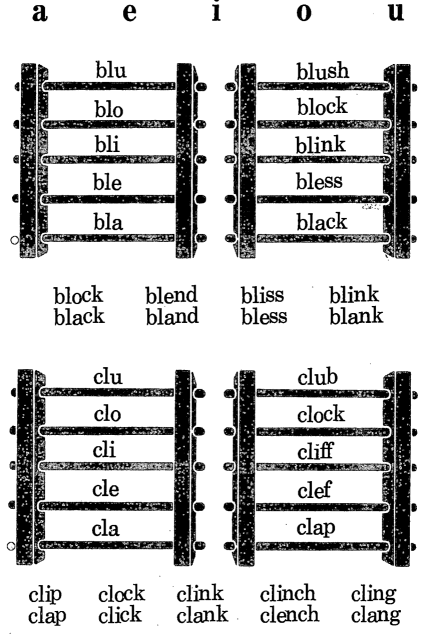

blu
blo
bli
ble
bla

blush
block
blink
bless
black

block	blend	bliss	blink
black	bland	bless	blank

clu
clo
cli
cle
cla

club
clock
cliff
clef
clap

clip	clock	clink	clinch	cling
clap	click	clank	clench	clang

a   e   i   o   u

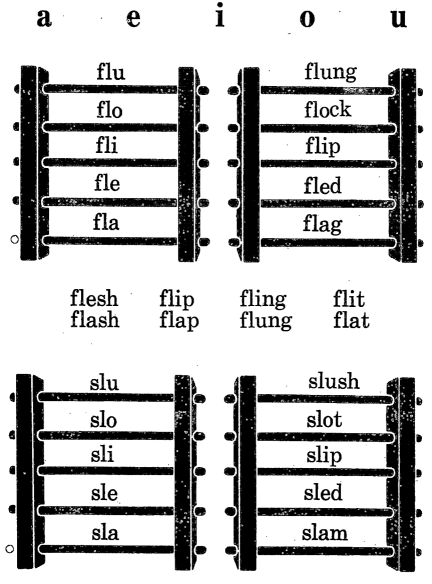

flu   flung
flo   flock
fli   flip
fle   fled
fla   flag

| flesh | flip | fling | flit |
| flash | flap | flung | flat |

slu   slush
slo   slot
sli   slip
sle   sled
sla   slam

| slip | slam | slush | slid |
| slap | slum | slash | sled |

a	e	i	o	u
plan	plum	plus	plot	
plant	plump	plush	plop	
glad	glass	gland	glum	

I will plant a plum tree.
I hope it has fat, plump plums.
Then, I will be glad.
If it has no plums,
I will be sad, or glum.

black	plan	class	flat
glad	slept	plant	sled
clap	slap	slip	clock
clip	glad	blush	block
flash	glass	cliff	fled
slid	cling	clung	slant

57

	a	**e**	**i**	**o**	**u**
1.	ca	ke	ki	co	cu
2.	sca	ske	ski	sco	scu
1.	ma	me	mi	mo	mu
2.	sma	sme	smi	smo	smu
1.	na	ne	ni	no	nu
2.	sna	sne	sni	sno	snu
1.	pa	pe	pi	po	pu
2.	spa	spe	spi	spo	spu
1.	ta	te	ti	to	tu
2.	sta	ste	sti	sto	stu
1.	wa	we	wi		
2.	swa	swe	swi	swo	swu

a   e   i   o   u

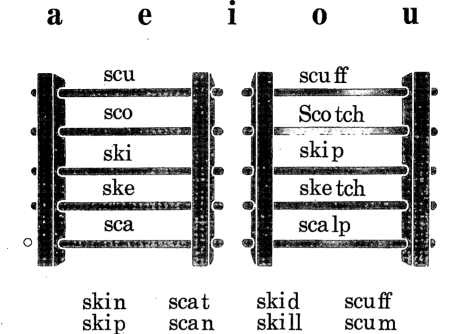

scu	scuff
sco	Scotch
ski	skip
ske	sketch
sca	scalp

skin   scat   skid   scuff
skip   scan   skill   scum

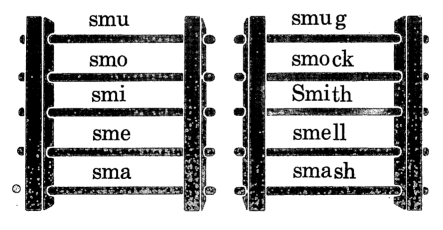

smu	smug
smo	smock
smi	Smith
sme	smell
sma	smash

smack   smelt

a e i o u

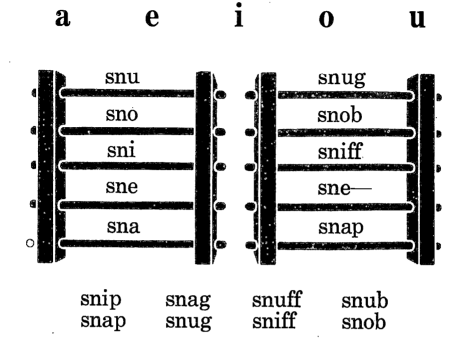

snu
sno
sni
sne
sna

snug
snob
sniff
sne—
snap

snip   snag   snuff   snub
snap   snug   sniff   snob

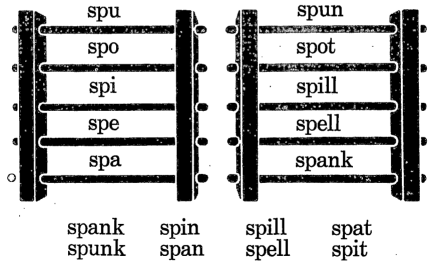

spu
spo
spi
spe
spa

spun
spot
spill
spell
spank

spank   spin   spill   spat
spunk   span   spell   spit

a e i o u

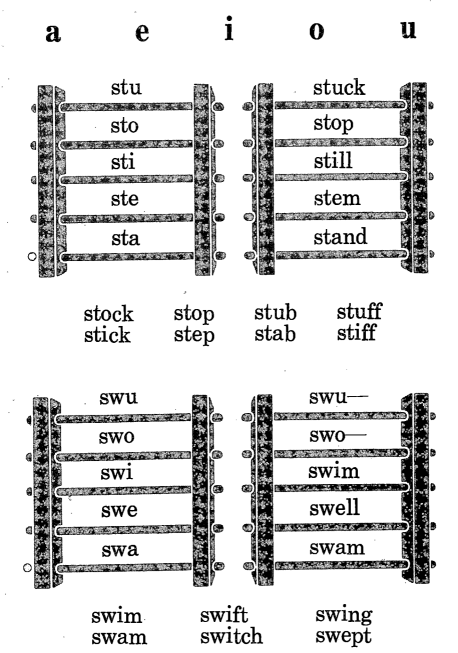

stu	stuck
sto	stop
sti	still
ste	stem
sta	stand

stock   stop   stub   stuff
stick   step   stab   stiff

swu	swu—
swo	swo—
swi	swim
swe	swell
swa	swam

swim   swift   swing
swam   switch   swept

swift	stand	swell	clap	clock
fling	slap	spin	slam	slip
plan	glad	plus	glass	glum
black	flag	block	scalp	smash
smock	skid	plant	flash	swim
		stamp	spank	stick
		swing	clip	bless

I fling myself on my sled.

Down the hill I fly.

Trees and houses flash by.

My sled is as swift as a jet.

Suddenly it begins to skid.

Smash! Into a stump I go.

I stop and spill into the snow.

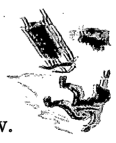

c a n

e

can	hat	mat	cap	back
can^e	hat^e	mat^e	cap^e	bak^e
sham	fat	rack	tap	sack
sham^e	fat^e	rak^e	tap^e	sak^e
pan	shack	mad	lack	tack
pan^e	shak^e	mad^e	lak^e	tak^e
Sam	fad	Pal	man	quack
sam^e	fad^e	pal^e	man^e	quak^e
cak^e	dat^e	cam^e	daz^e	lam^e
mak^e	gat^e	tam^e	gaz^e	flam^e
wak^e	lat^e	gam^e	haz^e	blam^e

me   he   she   we   be

63

rip	hid	shin	din	lick
ripe	hide	shine	dine	like
rid	pick	pin	fin	kit
ride	pike	pine	fine	kite
fill	Dick	bit	till	Tim
file	dike	bite	tile	time
mill	quit	mitt	dim	pill
mile	quite	mite	dime	pile
side	wife	wine	lime	dive
tide	life	mine	time	hive
wide	fife	nine	dime	five

mile	lime	tile	pike
smile	slime	stile	spike
pine	mite	wine	
spine	smite	swine	

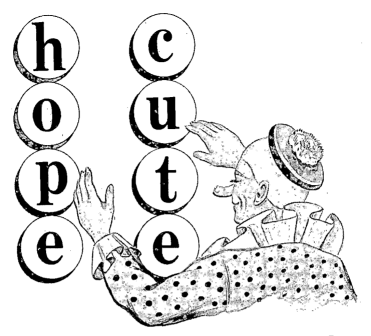

hop	rob	mop	tot	cod
hope	robe	mope	tote	code

pock	rod	dot	not	doll
poke	rode	dote	note	dole

hope	bone	poke	sole	mope
hole	lone	joke	pole	hope
home	tone	woke	mole	cope

tone	cone	lobe	poke	lope
stone	scone	globe	spoke	slope

cut	tub	duck	cub	dun
cute	tube	duke	cube	dune

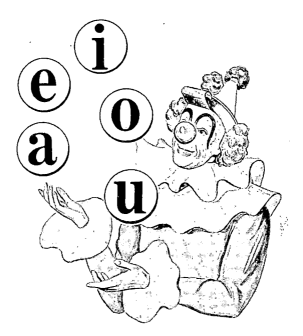

snake	rope	haste	time
those	tube	dive	hive
flame	safe	case	blaze
came	cube	tame	lame
like	dome	waste	quake
chase	plane	spoke	vase
vote	flake	while	taste
stole	paste	white	pipe
tune	glide	fine	poke
mule	slope	fake	bone
these	gave	save	size

1. rod	pane	like	dim
2. rode	pan	lick	dime
1. back	hope	ride	cut
2. bake	hop	rid	cute
1. note	shack	wine	pin
2. not	shake	win	pine
1. cube	doll	shine	Tim
2. cub	dole	shin	time
1. pale	tack	kite	tub
2. Pal	take	kit	tube
1. hat	same	hide	duck
2. hate	Sam	hid	duke
1. smoke	still	slide	spin
2. smock	stile	slid	spine
1. stoke	glad	plan	stake
2. stock	glade	plane	stack

old	told	cold	hold
sold	fold	scold	gold

colt	bolt	toll	most
volt	molt	roll	post

find	kind	rind	child
hind	mind	wind	wild

go	both	so	jolt	child
blind	no	bold	pint	told
mold	mild	grind	host	kind

	a	**e**	**i**	**o**	**u**
1.	ra	re	ri	ro	ru
2.	bra	bre	bri	bro	bru
1.	ra	re	ri	ro	ru
2.	cra	cre	cri	cro	cru
1.	ra	re	ri	ro	ru
2.	dra	dre	dri	dro	dru
1.	ra	re	ri	ro	ru
2.	fra	fre	fri	fro	fru
1.	ra	re	ri	ro	ru
2.	gra	gre	gri	gro	gru
1.	ra	re	ri	ro	ru
2.	pra	pre	pri	pro	pru
1.	ra	re	ri	ro	ru
2.	tra	tre	tri	tro	tru

a   e   i   o   u

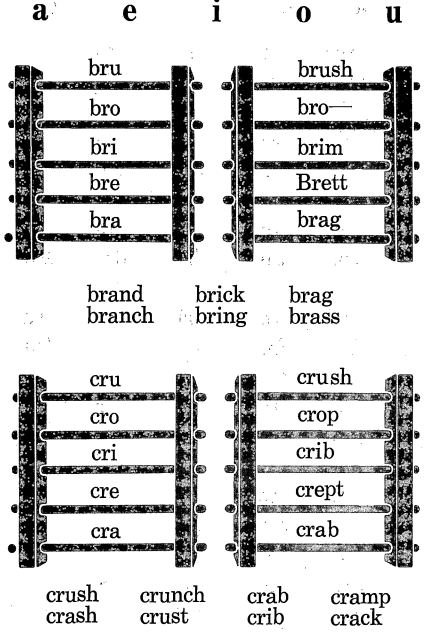

bru	brush	
bro	bro—	
bri	brim	
bre	Brett	
bra	brag	

brand   brick   brag
branch   bring   brass

cru	crush	
cro	crop	
cri	crib	
cre	crept	
cra	crab	

crush   crunch   crab   cramp
crash   crust   crib   crack

a   e   i   o   u

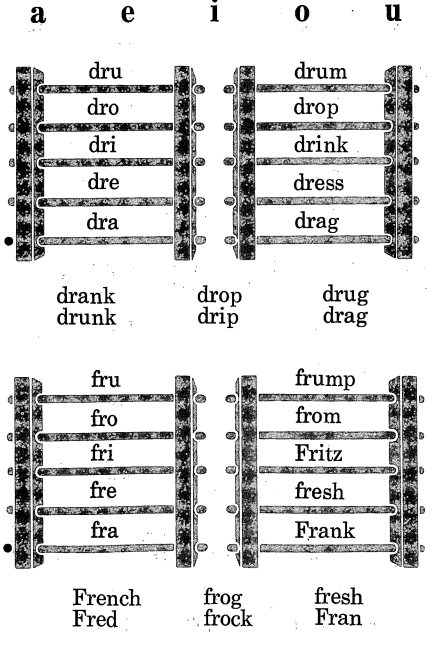

dru   drum
dro   drop
dri   drink
dre   dress
dra   drag

drank   drop   drug
drunk   drip   drag

fru   frump
fro   from
fri   Fritz
fre   fresh
fra   Frank

French   frog   fresh
Fred   frock   Fran

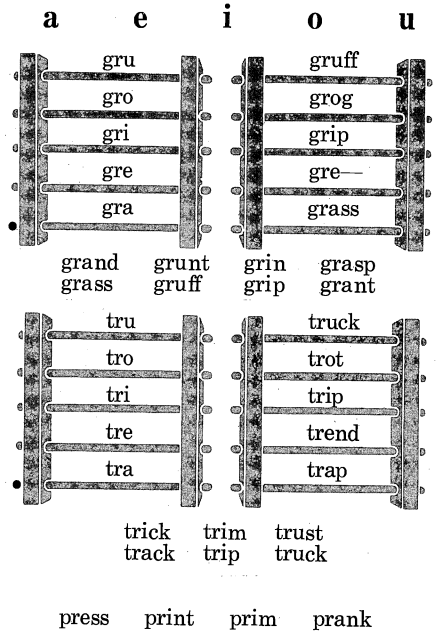

gru
gro
gri
gre
gra

gruff
grog
grip
gre—
grass

grand grunt grin grasp
grass gruff grip grant

tru
tro
tri
tre
tra

truck
trot
trip
trend
trap

trick trim trust
track trip truck

press print prim prank

72

grand	crisp	trade	bride
grill	print	grove	pride
frog	craze	graze	branch
dress	grunt	crack	truck
brave	brush	prize	drift
broke	bring	grape	crutch
tribe	frame	gruff	drill

rate	ride	rave	rove
crate	pride	brave	drove

robe	rake	rave	rate
probe	brake	crave	grate

broke	grove	drove
brake	grave	drive

prize	grave	trade	grape
prime	craze	grade	drape

run n ing

rub	run	pop
rubbing	running	popping
dig	hit	nap
digging	hitting	napping
dip	pin	win
dipping	pinning	winning
hum	hop	rob
humming	hopping	robbing

74

get	stop	chop
getting	stopping	chopping
shut	cut	pat
shutting	cutting	patting
slap	plan	skip
slapping	planning	skipping
spin	sit	let
spinning	sitting	letting

jump	help	stand
jumping	helping	standing
sing	think	pick
singing	thinking	picking
bring	send	print
bringing	sending	printing
tell	catch	pitch
telling	catching	pitching
spend	check	sell
spending	checking	selling

hide	hope	poke	take
hiding	hoping	poking	taking
wake	bake	ride	shine
waking	baking	riding	shining
bite	name	taste	chase
biting	naming	tasting	chasing
make	tame	gaze	rake
making	taming	gazing	raking
dine	joke	paste	doze
dining	joking	pasting	dozing
shake	like	hike	quake
shaking	liking	hiking	quaking

slide	blame	smoke	glide
sliding	blaming	smoking	gliding
drive	smile	trade	blaze
driving	smiling	trading	blazing
slope	brave	skate	grade
sloping	braving	skating	grading

grazing	drilling	framing	matching
dressing	hopping	hoping	stoning
flashing	hiding	printing	smashing
roping	spading	shaming	sketching
flaming	fussing	snipping	prizing

ar

| far | bar | chart | darn |
| farm | barn | charm | dark |

| park | mart | car | tar |
| spark | smart | scar | star |

or

| for | cord | porch | horn |
| fork | cork | torch | horse |

| scorn | storm | morn | born |
| scorch | stork | morning | torn |

er   ir   ur

er	ir	ur
her	sir	turn
herd	stir	burn
fern	girl	fur
jerk	dirt	curb
term	first	purr
clerk	birth	hurt
berth	third	curl

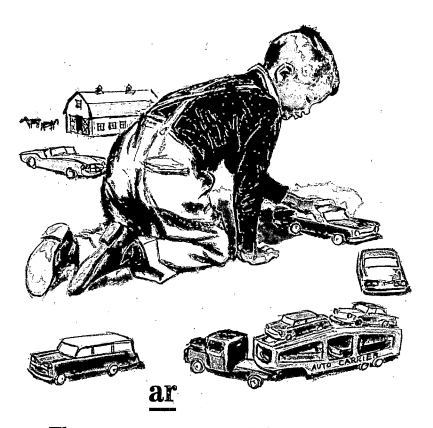

ar

These are my cars. I have big cars, little cars, long cars, short cars—even cars carting cars.

Where do my cars go? To market, to farm—past house and past barn. They march in a line. They stop. They start. Sometimes they part. Where do they go, all these cars?

Well, they go where I make them go!

or

One morning Rick went jogging along on his horse. He saw Nora on her porch.

"Good morning, Rick," said Nora. "What is the horse's name?"

"His name is North Wind. He is short, but he can fly like the wind."

"Will he fly if I toot my horn?"

"I cannot tell you."

So Nora tooted her horn. North Wind stopped short. Then, with a snort, he tore down the road.

"What sport it is to ride a horse!" said Rick.

er   ir   ur

It was Jane's third birthday. Her sister, Betty, was curling her hair.

"Turn this way. Then, I can curl the back of your hair," said Betty. "And do stand still. Don't jerk your head or stir a bit. You must be a pretty girl for the party."

"Will Bert come to my party?" asked Jane.

"Yes, and he will bring you a gift. I think it is a pretty purse."

bark	stern	mark	north
card	sport	nor	burst
jar	pork	shirt	mark
sharp	fort	park	part
term	sort	form	sore
form	yard	charm	dark
more	tore	store	score
wore	sore	nurse	purse

sit	spin	swim
sitter	spinner	swimmer
drum	plan	run
drummer	planner	runner
chop	cut	dip
chopper	cutter	dipper

help	jump	camp
helper	jumper	camper
send	start	mark
sender	starter	marker
pitch	catch	farm
pitcher	catcher	farmer

ride	trade	chase
rider	trader	chaser
drive	make	shake
driver	maker	shaker
bake	smoke	time
baker	smoker	timer

black	red	cute
blacker	redder	cuter
big	old	kind
bigger	older	kinder
brave	hot	cold
braver	hotter	colder

summer	winter	corner
supper	dinner	letter
ever	never	under
better	sister	mister

dinner	filing	hopping
diner	filling	hoping
cuter	snipping	mopping
cutter	sniping	moping

ai

rain	ail	rain	rail
train	fail	grain	trail
grain	wait	maid	fail
brain	wail	paid	jail
pain	tail	mail	laid
gain	sail	bail	raid

ay

lay	ray	way	lay
play	pray	sway	clay
day	pay	may	gay
say	gray	hay	Ray

stain	vain	way	pail
pray	slay	saint	chain
stay	tray	aid	aim
paint	faint	fail	gain
faith	plain	may	nail

ai   **ay**

One day, long ago and far away, a milkmaid was going to market. On her head was a pail of milk. As she went, she made plans.

"I shall sell my pail of milk. Maybe I shall get chickens. The chickens will lay eggs. By Christmas I will have a hundred. I shall sell them and get a dress. I shall look so pretty. Every one will want to walk with me. Shall I let them? No, I shall toss my head and say . . . "

Just then she did toss her head. And down went the pail! "No milk," she said sadly. "No milk, no chickens. No chickens, no eggs. No eggs, no dress."

84

ee

deed	tree	heed	peep
deep	free	heel	peek
see	fee	wee	bee
seed	feet	weed	beef
seen	feed	week	beet
seem	feel	weep	beech
sleep	fleet	sweep	meet
sleeve	sleet	sweet	need
greet	freeze	sheet	keep
green	breeze	sheep	keen

ea

sea	leap	cheat	tea
seat	lean	cheap	teach
eat	read	leaf	beat
east	real	leap	beast
each	reach	leave	beach
dream	bean	deal	feast
cream	mean	meal	least

ea ee

"Say what you mean!" the March Hare said.

"I do," Alice replied. "At least—at least I mean what I say. That is the same thing."

"Not the same thing a bit!" said the Hatter. "You might as well say that I see what I eat is the same as I eat what I see."

"You might as well say," added the March Hare, "that I like what I get is the same thing as I get what I like."

The Dormouse seemed to be talking in his sleep. "You might as well say that I breathe when I sleep is the same as I sleep when I breathe."

ie

lie	cries	cried	my	try
lies	dries	dried	by	cry
lied	tries	tried	fly	fry
tie	fries	fried	sly	dry
ties	spies	spied	ply	why
tied	pies	pie	sky	shy

y

(see above)

oa

load	road	soak	goat	coat
loaf	toad	soap	boat	coach
	roast	coast	float	
	toast	boast	throat	

oe

Joe	hoe	goes	woe
foe	hoed	toes	toe

ow

low	row	bow	tow
slow	grow	bowl	crow
flow	grown	throw	show
blow	growth	thrown	snow

hollow	fellow	willow	window
follow	yellow	pillow	shadow

<u>ie</u>   <u>y</u>

Beth has made a pie. It is a peach
pie.

"I made it for my mother," said Beth.
"I made a little pie for my kitten, too."

Bob said, "Your kitten will die if she
tries to eat that pie!"

Beth began to cry.

"Why, Beth! Don't cry," said Bob.
"I'll eat the pie so your kitten won't die."

oa   oe   ow

"I am going to a pet show," said Joe. "My wagon is a float. In the wagon is a bowl of water. In the bowl of water is a boat. And what do you think is on the boat? It is my pet toad."

"May I go to the pet show with you?" asked Joan. "I am taking my pet goat. Her name is Cocoa. I think she looks pretty with a yellow bow at her throat."

Do you think the toad or the goat will win a prize at the pet show?

read	breast	death	threat
bread	breath	dead	thread

health	dread	weather
wealth	tread	instead

thief	brief	believe
chief	field	relief
grief	yield	priest

way	far	sleep	side
away	afar	asleep	aside

while	drift	wake	like
awhile	adrift	awake	alike

part	head	jar	stir
apart	ahead	ajar	astir

woke	muse	rose	top
awoke	amuse	arose	atop

<u>ce</u>=<u>se</u>   <u>ci</u>=<u>si</u>   <u>cy</u>=<u>si</u>

cent	cell	cease	center
cider	civil	cinder	cyclone

ace	ice	face
pace	nice	race

lace	race	rice	pace
place	Grace	price	space
ice	spice	peace	trace
slice	twice	piece	brace

prince	since	hence	dance	chance
prance	mince	fence	dunce	France

niece	mice	cyclone	spice
peace	thence	fleece	place
princess	acid	pencil	cease
cinch	piece	twice	nice
ice	ace	thrice	circus
cigar	cider	cistern	decide

91

ce

"Grace, will you go to the store for me, please?" asked Mother.

"Yes," said Grace. "May I get some ice cream for dinner?"

"Indeed you may. If I can find a pencil, I shall jot down the other things we need."

This is the list that Grace's mother made: rice, slice of ham, can of mince meat, spice for pumpkin pie.

"Look at the price you pay for each thing," said Mother. "And do race back before the ice cream melts. Now, here is something nice for you. Ten cents to spend for anything you like."

ou

house	found	pound	shout
mouse	sound	round	scout
loud	round	out	about
cloud	ground	our	around

ow

how	down	gown	crowd
now	town	frown	crown
brown	growl	tower	power
drown	howl	flower	powder

oi

oil	toil	coin	point
boil	soil	join	joint

oy

boy	joy	toy	oyster
boys	joys	toys	oysters
voice	towel	cow	counter
mouth	coin	fowl	countess
sour	spoil	grouch	frown
count	choice	growl	Roy
counting	enjoy	moist	bounce

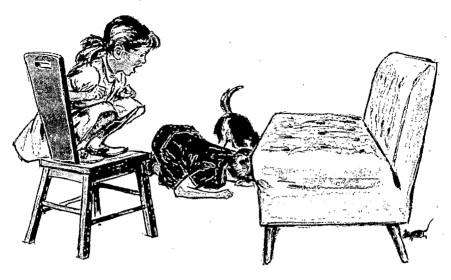

<u>ou</u>   <u>ow</u>

"A mouse! A mouse!" shouted Joyce.

"Where is the mouse, Joyce?" asked Roy.

"It is crouching under the couch."

"Sh! Cease your shouting! Don't make a sound. I will rout it out."

Roy chased the mouse around and around. Pal growled and chased the mouse, too. At last the mouse ran out of the house.

"Now, you can get down off the chair," said Roy. "Stop frowning. The little mouse has fled from the house."

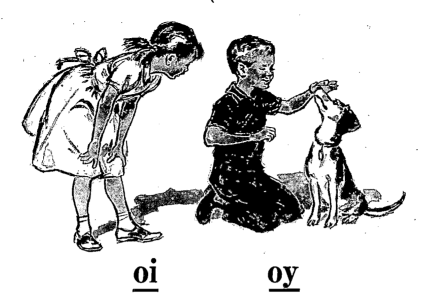

<u>oi</u>   <u>oy</u>

"Sit still, Pal! Be a good boy!" said Roy. "I am going to teach you a trick."

"Why are you teaching Pal a trick?" asked Joyce.

"I want him to win a prize in the pet show," said Roy. "I am going to teach him how to balance a coin on the point of his moist nose."

"Hold up a choice bit of meat. Then place the coin on his nose," said Joyce. "That's a fine idea," said Roy. "Would you like to join me in teaching Pal some tricks?"

"Yes," said Joyce. "I would enjoy that, but I don't think Pal would."

fun	gum	sun	dad
funny	gummy	sunny	daddy
Bob	Peg	Dan	Jim
Bobby	Peggy	Danny	Jimmy

dust	mess	soap	hill
dusty	messy	soapy	hilly
health	wealth	rain	sleep
healthy	wealthy	rainy	sleepy

bone	smoke	taste	wave
bony	smoky	tasty	wavy

puppy	daddy	lady	baby
puppies	daddies	ladies	babies
dolly	party	candy	penny
dollies	parties	candies	pennies

cooky	fairy	carry	silly
happy	cookies	carries	handy
twenty	armies	funny	fifty
army	fairies	funnies	thirty

sigh	right	thigh
sight	bright	light
tight	fight	slight
night	fright	flight
might	high	plight

not   night
knot   knight

knee   knife   know   knelt
kneel   knit   known   knock

right   ring
write   wring

wreck   wrong   write   wreath
wring   wrist   wrote   wretch

often   listen   hasten
soften   glisten   chasten

limb   comb   dumb   debt
lamb   climb   thumb   doubt

j

jam	jig	job	just
jump	joke	jest	Jean
James	Jane	Jack	jail

ge=j sound

change   range   engage

lunge   hinge   plunge   fringe

age	huge	sage	cage
wage	page	rage	stage

large   barge   charge   urge

dge=j sound

edge	ridge	badge	judge
ledge	fudge	dodge	bridge
hedge	lodge	wedge	Madge
pledge	budge	smudge	nudge

oo

coo	food	too	toot	goose
cool	fool	tool	tooth	loose
stool	spoon	droop	boost	boot
stoop	spool	troop	roost	booth
bloom	roof	room	zoo	soon
groom	proof	doom	shoot	moon

oo

cook	look	hoof	good
book	took	hook	hood
wool	soot	crook	shook
wood	foot	brook	stood

foolish	noonday	woolen
moonlight	goodness	papoose
smooth	wooden	cooler
looking	cooker	sooner
footstep	boot	cooking
teaspoon	toothbrush	scooping
fooling	roomer	hooking
stool	footstool	groom
mood	tooting	booklet
gloom	scooter	coolness

oo

"The gray goose has been loose since noon," said Mike. "Help me find her, Patty."

"Did you look in the chicken coop? Maybe she is roosting with the chickens."

"She is a foolish goose, I know. But she would not go to the chicken coop."

"Maybe she went to the barn for food."

"I have been there, too, but no goose."

"I see her, Mike! She is hiding under the porch stoop. She is a foolish goose! She wanted us to play hide-and-seek with her."

00

Pinocchio was a puppet made of wood.

One day he fell asleep near a fire. His wooden feet began to burn.

He awoke, took one look, and cried, "Goodness! What shall I do? I have a right foot but no left foot!"

He shook as he cried. "A right foot, but no left foot."

Just then his father came in. "Stop crying, Pinocchio. I can make you a left foot out of a wooden spoon."

ew   ue

blew	drew	threw	blue	true
flew	grew	chew	flue	glue

ew

new	few	pew	stew
news	dew	mew	anew

ue

due	sue	hue

flute	prune	rule	plume
Judy	Jupiter	rude	brute

few	mew	threw	news
clue	grew	chew	pew
hue	blue	true	brew
crew	due	blew	glue

aw

saw	law	paw	dawn
jaw	lawn	draw	yawn
hawk	crawl	shawl	thaw

au

haul	pause	clause	sauce	caught
Paul	cause	fault	Maud	taught

al

halt   false   salt   bald   malt

all

ball	tall	wall	fall
call	stall	hall	small

daughter	also	already
salty	almost	crawler
crawling	caller	crawling
pausing	smaller	yawning
causing	taller	calling
drawing	halting	faun

au   aw

Paul and Maud were sitting on the lawn.

Paul said, "Let's play Indians. I will be a Shawnee chief. My name will be Hawk Eye."

"I will be your squaw," said Maud. "My name will be Bright Dawn. My doll will be our daughter. I'll call her Little Fawn."

"I must daub some paint on my face to look like a real Indian," said Paul.

"I will put on a shawl," said Maud.

Soon Mother came out.

She said, "My, my. Let's see what fine Indian scouts you are. Dig out all the weeds in this lawn."

al   all

There was once an unhappy circus pony. He was unhappy because people called him Half-Pint.

Half-Pint did not like the tall clowns. When they rode him, they made him feel so very, very small. He would halt, and they would fall. They would put him in his stall, and he would kick the wall all day.

The tall clowns always fooled him. They would give him salt instead of a lump of sugar.

se = z sound

chose	wise	praise
rose	these	please
nose	those	ease
pose	cheese	tease
pause	cause	noise
choose	because	rise

ph = f sound

telephone	nephew	pamphlet
prophet	phrase	photograph
elephant	orphan	telegraph
Philip	phone	phonograph

middle	handle	wiggle
bundle	battle	puzzle
sample	circle	little
buckle	tickle	pickle

ream	ray	rap	rain
cream	pray	trap	train
scream	spray	strap	strain

screen	spring	street	splash
scrub	sprinkle	straw	splendid
scrap	spread	stream	split
scrape	spray	strike	splint
scratch	sprang	strip	splatter

| row | rash | rust | rice |
| throw | thrash | thrust | thrice |

| thrill | throat | thread | three |

scribble	struggle	scratching
scramble	threaten	streamer
sprinkle	threw	strainer
straight	thrown	strapping
stranger	splitting	spruce
stroke	scrubbing	thrush
strong	throne	stretch
struck	thrice	splinter

tion
sion = shun sound

station	addition	mission
nation	affection	impression
portion	action	expression

education	population	attention
vacation	invitation	section
promotion	foundation	mention

or = er sound

actor	visitor	sailor	editor
major	razor		error
labor	harbor		janitor
favor	armor		elevator
humor	debtor		mirror
author	splendor		donor

ed

taste	start	paint
tasted	started	painted
seat	fold	waste
seated	folded	wasted
light	print	trust
lighted	printed	trusted
shout	add	part
shouted	added	parted
plant	end	state
planted	ended	stated
need	land	act
needed	landed	acted
count	trade	toast
counted	traded	toasted
point	sight	wait
pointed	sighted	waited
crowd	list	sound
crowded	listed	sounded
rest	note	shade
rested	noted	shaded

ed = d sound

name	allow	change
named	allowed	changed
kill	burn	trail
killed	burned	trailed
play	enter	save
played	entered	saved
plan	rain	gain
planned	rained	gained
roll	fill	harm
rolled	filled	harmed
dream	pin	join
dreamed	pinned	joined
call	sail	fail
called	sailed	failed
turn	follow	stay
turned	followed	stayed
aim	form	lean
aimed	formed	leaned

ed = t sound

kiss	wish	thank
kissed	wished	thanked
reach	march	shape
reached	marched	shaped
race	talk	splash
raced	talked	splashed
box	place	shock
boxed	placed	shocked
hatch	rope	smoke
hatched	roped	smoked
pitch	pack	mark
pitched	packed	marked
kick	pick	hope
kicked	picked	hoped
bake	stretch	look
baked	stretched	looked
stop	stamp	like
stopped	stamped	liked
camp	skip	jump
camped	skipped	jumped

1. kiss   miss   fuss
   kissed   missed   fussed
   hiss   bless   gas
   hissed   blessed   gassed

2. puff   stuff   sniff
   puffed   stuffed   sniffed
   huff   cuff   snuff
   huffed   cuffed   snuffed

3. hatch   pitch   hitch
   hatched   pitched   hitched
   fetch   patch   stretch
   fetched   patched   stretched

4. reach   poach   bleach
   reached   poached   bleached
   march   perch   preach
   marched   perched   preached

5. peck　　　wink　　　mark
   pecked　　winked　　marked
   smoke　　bake　　　like
   smoked　　baked　　liked

6. kick　　　quack　　stack
   kicked　　quacked　stacked
   crack　　back　　　wreck
   cracked　backed　　wrecked

7. pace　　　mince　　price
   paced　　minced　　priced
   slice　　trace　　lace
   sliced　　traced　　laced

8. stop　　　tip　　　trip
   stopped　tipped　　tripped
   skip　　　tap　　　flap
   skipped　tapped　　flapped

9. wish   flash   fish

wished   flashed   fished

smash   hush   splash

smashed   hushed   splashed

10. box   wax   fix

boxed   waxed   fixed

vex   mix   relax

vexed   mixed   relaxed

thanked	named	shouted
wished	played	counted
kicked	filled	crowded
reached	changed	added
picked	sailed	rested
stepped	aimed	acted
marched	dreamed	landed
pitched	called	printed
hoped	rained	waited
looked	smiled	folded
smoked	turned	painted

bare	fare	rare	spare
care	hare	share	snare
dare	mare	stare	parent

air	fair	pair	stair
chair	hair	lair	flair

One fine, fair day Clair and Jim went to the airport. Their parents took them. They climbed the stairs to the roof. From the roof, they saw big airplanes land and take off.

A jet was preparing for a flight.

"Where will it go?" asked Clair.

"It is going to Paris," said Father.

"I would not care to go that far," said Clair.

"I would care to and also dare to," said Jim.

a/bout	ba/by	doc/tor
ac/tion	bat/tle	east/ern
ad/dress	bet/ter	em/ploy
a/fraid	bor/der	emp/ty
a/gree	bot/tle	en/gage
a/larm	but/ter	en/joy
al/most	cab/in	en/ter
al/so	can/not	es/cape
a/mount	cat/tle	eve/ning
ap/ple	cen/ter	ev/er
ap/ply	chap/ter	ex/cuse
ap/proach	chick/en	ex/pect
a/round	cir/cle	ex/pense
ar/rive	cit/y	ex/plain
art/ist	cor/ner	fair/ly
at/tack	dai/ly	farm/er
at/tempt	dark/ness	far/ther
au/thor	daugh/ter	fa/vor
a/void	din/ner	fel/low
a/way	dis/play	fif/teen

fif/ty	in/vite	mur/mur
fin/ish	it/self	my/self
flow/er	la/bor	nar/row
fol/low	lead/er	na/tion
for/est	lit/tle	nei/ther
for/mer	low/er	nev/er
fun/ny	ly/ing	no/ble
fur/nish	man/ner	north/ern
fur/ther	mat/ter	num/ber
gath/er	may/be	on/ly
go/ing	meet/ing	or/der
hab/it	mem/ber	out/side
her/self	men/tion	o/ver
him/self	mid/night	own/er
hur/ry	might/y	pa/per
in/crease	mis/take	part/ly
in/deed	mod/ern	par/ty
in/side	morn/ing	per/fect
in/sist	mo/tion	per/haps
in/tend	mur/der	per/mit

plen/ty	set/tle	trem/ble
pock/et	shad/ow	twen/ty
por/tion	shel/ter	un/der
pow/der	sil/ver	un/known
pow/er	sim/ple	un/less
prob/lem	sis/ter	un/til
prof/it	slow/ly	val/ue
prop/er	splen/did	vir/tue
pub/lish	sta/tion	weath/er
pu/pil	storm/y	west/ern
quick/ly	strug/gle	wheth/er
rail/road	sub/ject	whis/tle
read/y	suf/fer	will/ing
riv/er	sum/mer	win/dow
safe/ty	sur/prise	win/ter
sail/or	ta/ble	with/in
sav/ing	teach/er	with/out
scat/ter	ten/der	wit/ness
se/cret	thir/ty	writ/er
sec/tion	tick/et	yel/low

ac /ci /dent
ac /cord /ing
ad /di /tion
ad /ver /tise
af /fec /tion
aft /er /noon
A /lad /din
al /pha /bet
a /maz /ing
am /bi /tion
an /i /mals
ap /pe /tite
ar /gu /ment
ar /ti /cle
At /lan /tic
at /ten /tion
at /ti /tude
av /e /nue
be /long /ing
bi /cy /cle

but /ter /fly
cab /i /net
cal /en /dar
car /pen /ter
cel /e /brate
Co /lum /bus
com /mit /tee
com /pan /ion
con /di /tion
con /sid /er
con /tin /ue
dav /en /port
De /cem /ber
de /cid /ed
de /ci /sion
dif /fer /ent
dif /fi /cult
di /vi /sion
eas /i /ly
e /lec /tric

el /e /phant
e /lev /en
en /e /mies
en /ter /tain
es /tab /lish
ex /cep /tion
ex /act /ly
ex /cel /lent
ex /er /cise
fam /i /ly
fol /low /ing
for /ev /er
gar /den /ing
hap /pi /ness
hes /i /tate
hol /i /day
hos /pi /tal
how /ev /er
hur /ri /cane
im /i /tate

im /por /tant

in /di /cate

in /dus /try

in /tro /duce

in /ven /tion

in /vit /ed

jan /i /tor

lib /er /ty

lo /ca /tion

min /is /ter

mis /tak /en

mo /tor /boat

na /tion /al

news /pa /per

no /bod /y

No /vem /ber

now /a /days

oc /ca /sion

Oc /to /ber

oc /to /pus

o /ver /eat

o /ver /look

pas /sen /ger

per /fect /ly

pop /u /lar

pos /si /ble

po /ta /to

prac /ti /cal

pre /tend /ed

prob /a /bly

prop /er /ly

re /la /tion

re /mem /ber

rep /re /sent

sac /ri /fice

sat /is /fy

Sat /ur /day

sep /a /rate

Sep /tem /ber

sev /en /teen

sev /en /ty

slip /per /y

sud /den /ly

tax /i /cab

tel /e /gram

tel /e /phone

tel /e /scope

ter /ri /ble

to /geth /er

to /mor /row

trav /el /er

un /a /ble

un /hap /py

u /ni /form

un /luck /y

va /ca /tion

vac /ci /nate

val /en /tine

when /ev /er

yes /ter /day

bun	lap	bag	boast
barn	lip	big	best
burn	loop	bug	baste
born	leap	beg	Bert

sing	spark	top	mad
sang	speak	tap	mud
song	spoke	tip	maid
sung	spook	tape	made

rip	while	check	deck
rap	wheel	cheek	dock
ripe	whale	chick	Dick
rope	whirl	choke	duck

flirt	steal	sleep	drape
flat	stole	slip	drop
fleet	stale	slap	drip
float	stool	slope	droop

bad	bet	fat	back
bed	beat	fit	bake
bud	bat	fate	bike
bid	but	feet	book
bird	bit	foot	beak

fad	cap	fan	lit
fed	cape	fin	let
feed	coop	fine	lot
fade	cop	fern	late
ford	cup	fun	loot

Sam	cheap	toil	had
sum	chip	tell	hid
same	chap	tale	herd
seem	chirp	tail	hide
seam	chop	tool	hard

God	room	spoil	trip
good	roam	spool	trap

cat	mile	tame	tick
cot	mill	time	tock
cute	mail	Tim	tack
cart	male	Tom	tuck
coat	meal	team	take
cut	mule	term	took
sat	ban	sell	hat
seat	bone	sill	hate
sit	burn	sale	heat
set	barn	sail	hoot
salt	born	sole	hurt
site	bean	soil	halt
sack	man	dad	hill
sick	men	dead	heel
sock	mean	deed	heal
suck	morn	died	hail
sake	moan	did	hole
seek	main	dud	haul
soak	moon	dude	hurl

rode	mat	lack	fall
red	mate	lick	fail
rid	meet	lock	feel
ride	mitt	luck	fell
raid	might	leak	fill
rod	met	like	file
read	mart	lake	fool
road	meat	look	foil
lad	ring	pat	pail
led	wring	pet	pale
laid	right	pit	peel
lid	write	pot	pal
lead	rap	part	pile
load	wrap	port	pole
lied	root	Pete	pool
knot	steak	pick	will
not	stack	park	well
night	stick	pork	wall
knight	stuck	pack	wail
knit	stock	peck	wool

peach	spine	star	shack
pitch	spin	store	shake
patch	span	stir	shook
porch	spun	stare	shark

claim	lawn	noise	rule
climb	lane	nose	rail
clam	loan	knows	role

short	miss	for	stair
shoot	mess	fare	star
shot	mass	far	store
shirt	muss	fair	stir

shape	torn	loud	bowl
ship	tin	led	bill
sheep	tan	lad	bell
sharp	turn	load	ball
shop	tone	lied	boil

him	must	goat	groan
harm	mist	got	grin
home	mast	gate	grain
Spain	strap	farm	trick
spoon	strip	foam	track
spine	stripe	form	truck
coast	base	band	fond
cost	Bess	bend	found
cast	bus	bind	find
goat	stuff	slam	spill
got	stiff	slum	spell
gate	staff	slim	spoil
rack	peel	scar	girl
rock	pile	scare	gull
rake	pole	score	goal

Sight Words

again	father	one	two
along	four	only	very
any	full	pretty	walk
are	give	pull	want
been	goes	put	warm
both	have	said	was
buy	here	shall	wash
come	laugh	some	were
could	live	talk	what
do	long	the	where
does	many	their	who
done	mother	there	work
don't	of	they	would
eight	off	to	you
everyone	once	today	your